WHALE SHARK

By Martha London

Consultant: Erin McCo[...]
Educator, Aquarium of the [...]

Minneapolis, Minnesota

Credits

Cover and title page, © Cultura Creative RF/Alamy, © djgis/Shutterstock, © Yuri Samsonov/Shutterstock; 3, © nabil refaat/Shutterstock; 4-5, © mihtiander/iStockPhoto; 6-7, © Nature Picture Library/Alamy; 8-9, © armiblue/iStockPhoto; 10-11, © VisionDive/Shutterstock; 11, © Napat/Shutterstock; 12, © Fat Jackey/Shutterstock; 12-13, © David Fleetham/Alamy; 14-15, © richcarey/iStockPhoto; 16-17, © Stocktrek Images, Inc./Alamy; 18-19, © wildestanimal/Getty; 20-21, © Andrea Izzotti/iStockPhoto; 22, © crisod/iStockPhoto; 22-23, © nabil refaat/Shutterstock; 24, © nabil refaat/Shutterstock.

President: Jen Jenson
Director of Product Development: Spencer Brinker
Senior Editor: Allison Juda
Associate Editor: Charly Haley
Designer: Colin O'Dea

Library of Congress Cataloging-in-Publication Data

Names: London, Martha, author.
Title: Whale shark / by Martha London.
Description: Minneapolis, Minnesota : Bearport Publishing Company, [2022] | Series: Shark shock! | Includes bibliographical references and index.
Identifiers: LCCN 2021030946 (print) | LCCN 2021030947 (ebook) | ISBN 9781636915357 (library binding) | ISBN 9781636915449 (paperback) | ISBN 9781636915531 (ebook)
Subjects: LCSH: Whale shark--Juvenile literature.
Classification: LCC QL638.95.R4 L66 2022 (print) | LCC QL638.95.R4 (ebook) | DDC 597.3/3--dc23
LC record available at https://lccn.loc.gov/2021030946
LC ebook record available at https://lccn.loc.gov/2021030947

Copyright © 2022 Bearport Publishing Company. All rights reserved. No part of this publication may be reproduced in whole or in part, stored in any retrieval system, or transmitted in any form or by any means, electronic, mechanical, photocopying, recording, or otherwise, without written permission from the publisher.

For more information, write to Bearport Publishing, 5357 Penn Avenue South, Minneapolis, MN 55419. Printed in the United States of America.

CONTENTS

Slow and Steady 4
Large and In Charge 6
In Warm Waters 8
A Tiny Meal 10
Filter Fun......................... 12
The Big, Friendly Giants........... 14
Harmful Humans 16
Pups in the Water 18
Growing Large 20

More about Whale Sharks 22
Glossary.......................... 23
Index............................. 24
Read More........................ 24
Learn More Online 24
About the Author.................. 24

Slow and Steady

A whale shark makes its way through warm ocean waters. The huge animal is on the hunt. It slowly opens its giant mouth and gulps. Tiny plants and animals are swept into the shark's mouth along with the water. Dinner is served in one tasty swallow!

The whale shark is the largest fish in the ocean, but it eats some of the smallest animals in the water.

Large and In Charge

A whale shark's wide, flat head helps it catch a lot of tiny **prey** at once. But that's just one end of an extremely large body. Huge fins and a large **forked** tail help the massive fish swim. The blue-gray shark is about 40 feet (12 m) long—the size of a school bus!

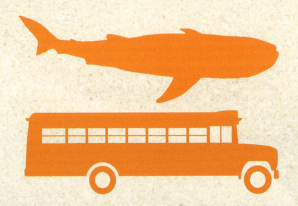

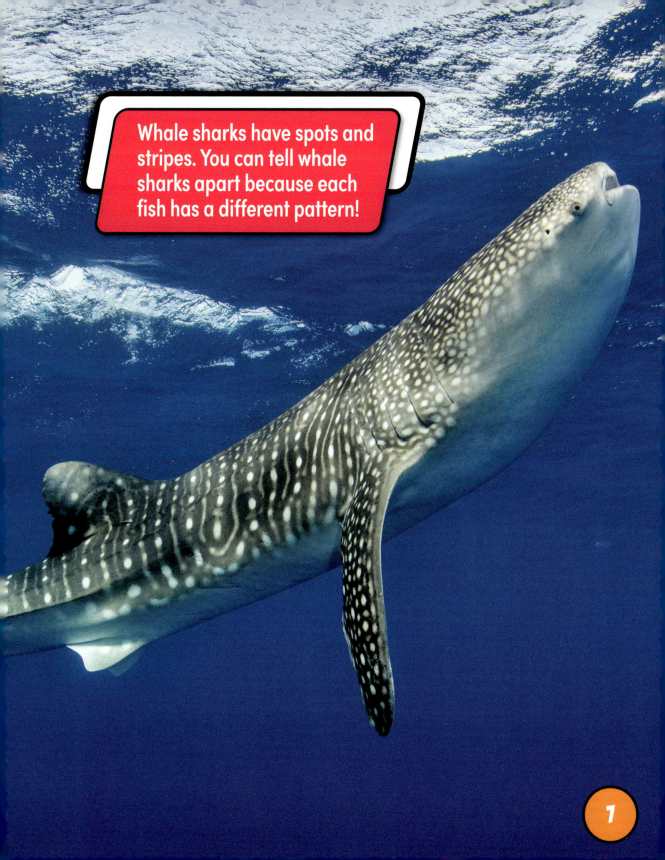

Whale sharks have spots and stripes. You can tell whale sharks apart because each fish has a different pattern!

In Warm Waters

These huge sharks swim in warm ocean waters near the **equator**. Because they are **cold-blooded**, whale sharks need heat in the water to stay warm. They also keep warm by being on the move. Whale sharks are rarely in one place for long. As they go, they often swim near the **surface** of the water.

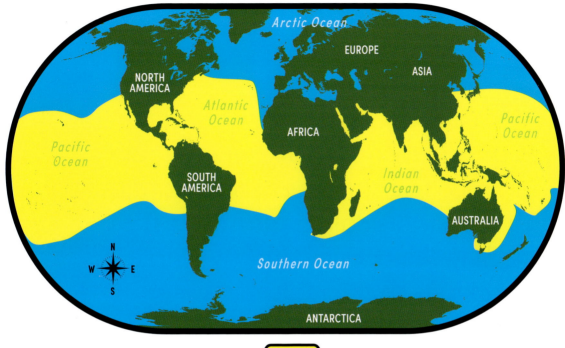

WHALE SHARKS AROUND THE WORLD

Where whale sharks live

Scientists think whale sharks swim about 17 miles (27 km) every day!

A Tiny Meal

Whale sharks swim at the surface for a good reason. That's where their food is! The sharks eat tiny plants and animals called **plankton** that float in the ocean. Hungry whale sharks swim through the water with open mouths to catch their meals.

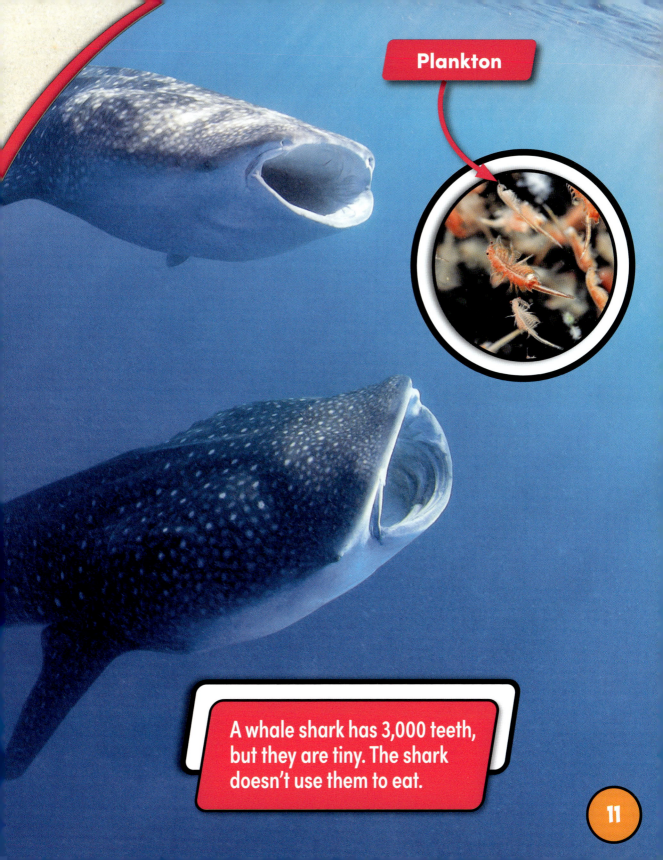

Plankton

A whale shark has 3,000 teeth, but they are tiny. The shark doesn't use them to eat.

Filter Fun

The whale shark is a **filter feeder**. It swims through the water with its huge mouth open. The water and plankton pass over a special part of the mouth that catches the plankton. Then, the water exits out through the shark's **gills**. The whale shark swallows its meal.

A whale shark's throat is only about the size of a quarter!

The Big, Friendly Giants

Although whale sharks are huge, they leave most of the other animals in the ocean alone. Their size also keeps them safe from harm. These sharks don't have many natural **predators**.

Sometimes the giants even help other animals. Smaller fish swim close to whale sharks. Since predators stay away from the huge whale sharks, the smaller fish are safe, too.

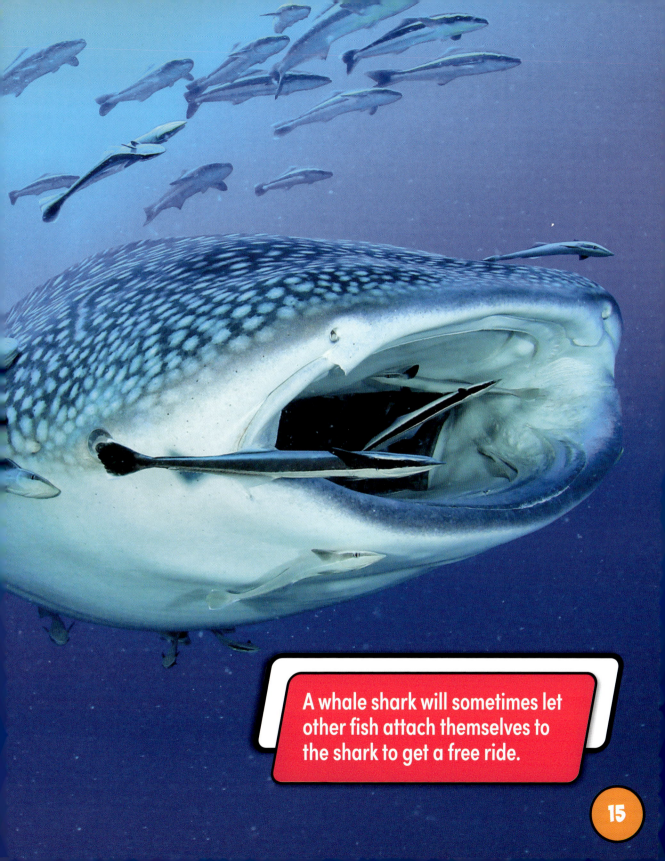

A whale shark will sometimes let other fish attach themselves to the shark to get a free ride.

Harmful Humans

The biggest dangers whale sharks face come from humans. Boats can sometimes run over the sharks and cut them. Most fishers do not hunt whale sharks, but they may trap them accidentally while using nets to catch other fish. The nets keep the sharks from swimming. And when sharks cannot swim, they also cannot eat or breathe.

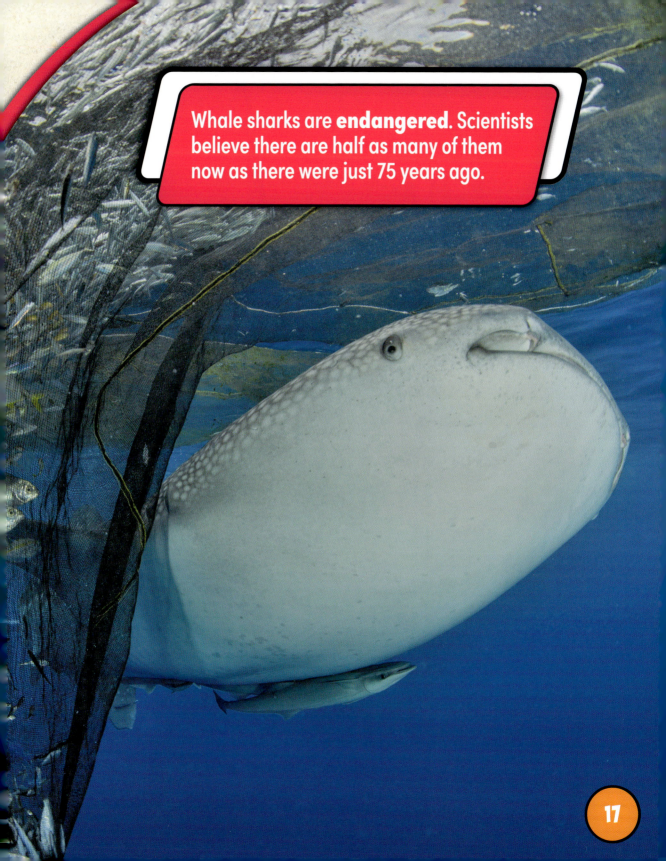

Whale sharks are **endangered**. Scientists believe there are half as many of them now as there were just 75 years ago.

Pups in the Water

Whale sharks spend most of their time alone. But sometimes they come together to **mate**. The shark babies, called pups, grow in eggs inside a **female** shark. Pups hatch from the eggs inside her. Then, the female shark gives birth to live young. Some scientists think a whale shark may have hundreds of pups at a time.

Whale sharks may also come together when there is a lot of food in one place.

Growing Large

Whale shark pups start out small. They are about 2 ft (0.6 m) long when they are born and grow only 1 ft (0.3 m) each year. Whale sharks are adults by the time they are about 30 years old. Then, they can have their own babies.

Whale sharks can live to be 100 years old.

More about Whale Sharks

Whale sharks have hundreds of tiny scales on their eyes. These growths act like armor to keep things from hurting the sharks' eyes.

A fully grown whale shark weighs more than three elephants.

Whale sharks swim only about as fast as most humans walk.

While they often stay close to the surface, whale sharks can also dive down thousands of feet deep.

Whale sharks sometimes suck in water and plankton like a vacuum!

A whale shark's skin is about 4 inches (10 cm) thick.

Glossary

cold-blooded having a body temperature that changes with the temperature of the environment

endangered in danger of dying out completely

equator the imaginary line around the middle of Earth

female a whale shark that can give birth to young

filter feeder an animal that takes food from water in order to eat

forked divided into two parts at one end; shaped like the letter Y

gills the parts of a fish that allow it to breathe underwater

mate to come together to have young

plankton tiny animals and plants that float in oceans and lakes

predators animals that hunt and eat other animals

prey animals that are hunted by other animals

surface the top layer of something, such as an ocean or river

Index

cold-blooded 8
eat 5, 10–11, 16
endangered 17
equator 8
filter feeder 12
humans 16, 22
mate 18
plankton 10, 12, 22
predators 14
prey 6
pups 18, 20
tail 6
teeth 11

Read More

Shea, Therese. *Whale Shark: The Largest Fish (Animal Record Breakers).* New York: PowerKids Press, 2020.

Twiddy, Robin. *Whale Shark (Teeth to Tail).* New York: KidHaven Publishing, 2020.

Learn More Online

1. Go to **www.factsurfer.com** or scan the QR code below.
2. Enter "**Whale Shark**" into the search box.
3. Click on the cover of this book to see a list of websites.

About the Author

Martha London lives in Minnesota with her cat. She's written more than 100 books for young readers!